I WILL GIVE YOU A NEW HEART

A REGNUM CHRISTI ESSAY ON THE DEVOTION TO THE SACRED HEART OF JESUS, AND ITS IMPORTANCE, MEANING, AND IMPLICATIONS FOR THE REGNUM CHRISTI MOVEMENT

FR. BRUCE WREN, LC

ISBN-10: 1986060608

ISBN-13: 978-1986060608

TABLE OF CONTENTS

I WILL GIVE YOU
A NEW HEART

PREFACE

In early March of 2017, the organizing committee for the Regnum Christi Formator's Convention at the University of St. Mary of the Lake in Mundelein, Illinois, asked me if I would be willing to give the opening meditation. They informed me that I could choose the theme, but that it should touch upon the fundamentals of Regnum Christi spirituality, and so serve as a sort of spiritual entrance into the themes that were to follow.

The meditation that I gave was intentionally written for that purpose: to propose an element of our spirituality as *foundational* for the Regnum Christi Movement. The meditation arose from the conviction that in all things, but even more so in the spiritual life, order is of utmost importance. If we do not have the first things right—the foundations—then nearly nothing that follows will be right. Perhaps it would be more precise to say that a few things might turn out okay, but the results will always end up being, at best, a bit askew.

A very common example will help to illustrate this point: the well-known board game Monopoly. At the table there is a player who, for some reason, really likes the railroads. He has such a fondness for them that he will do almost anything to obtain all four. Now all Monopoly players know that, in itself, this is a good thing: having the four railroads will certainly help one's chances of victory. However, if the goal of obtaining the four railroads comes *first* in a player's mind then, although he may make many prudent Monopoly-type decisions along the way and perhaps end up obtaining all four, he will probably not win the game. If our player does not have *first* in his mind to *win the game*, he may finally obtain his railroads, but only at the cost of one of his opponents scooping up Boardwalk, Park Place, and that dangerous green monopoly of Pennsylvania, North Carolina, and Pacific Avenues in the meantime. Our player will lose: the foundations of his Monopoly strategy were askew, and thus his decisions were disordered, misaligned, and unfruitful.

In somewhat the same way, attempting to arrive at a comprehension of the fundamental elements of our Regnum Christi spirituality is essential to its fruitful development. It is, however, much more problematic than a board game. This is especially so because of our history, so interwoven in the tumultuous and sadly often scandalous history of the founder of the Movement. All institutions in the Church must constantly look to reform themselves, to purify themselves from human error in order to return to the clarity of the original divinely inspired spirit which God gave their institutions. Indeed, the Church herself recognizes the need to be in constant reformation.[1] Still, if this discernment is necessary for all institutions in the Church, it is even more so for the Regnum Christi Movement, given our almost unique place in ecclesial history.

The talk I gave at the aforementioned Convention was my attempt to elucidate what is most fundamental in Regnum Christi spirituality. Each person must arrive to

---

1   Cfr. *Lumen Gentium* 8. The now well-known phrase of "*Ecclesia semper reformanda*" is of dubious origin and is often used by Protestant theologians for obvious reasons. It is, nevertheless, legitimized by the words of *Lumen Gentium*: *Ecclesia… sancta simul et semper purificanda, poenitentiam et renovationem continuo prosequitur* (the Church… at the same time holy and always in need of being purified, always follows the way of penance and renewal).

any truth, and a personal conviction about it, in a very personal and multi-dimensional way. I, too, took my own road, made up of prayer, study, and life experiences. The end result was that I could not come up with anything more fundamental and simpler than the devotion to the Sacred Heart of Jesus as the foundation of Regnum Christi spirituality, and thus of the Movement itself. Psalm 11:3 states: *If foundations are destroyed, what can the just one do?* The answer is: very little indeed.

This essay is a development of that original meditation given in March of 2017 in Mundelein. Who could doubt that if we give our best energies to the first things in our spiritual life, God will not fail to bless us?

FOREWORD: WHAT ARE RC ESSAYS?

RC Essays are extended, in-depth reflections on particular aspects of life as a Regnum Christi member. An Essay may develop the nature of a virtue, showing what that virtue might look like when lived out in harmony with the Regnum Christi identity and mission. An Essay may explore the challenges of living out one of the commitments shared by all members. An Essay may be instructive, explaining the history, context, and meaning of certain Movement traditions. In short, RC Essays are a chance for all of us to delve deeper into our charism, reflecting seriously on our spiritual patrimony, which the Church has recognized and lauded, and in that way helping that patrimony grow and bear fruit.

RC Essays make no pretense of being the sole and exhaustive expression of our charism. The RC Spirituality Center will review and edit them to ensure their quality in expression and content, but no single person owns a collective charism in such a way as to give it a definitive and exhaustive expression. This is one of the important lessons we have begun to learn in our process of reform and renewal.

Some RC Essays will lend themselves naturally to personal meditation; others will be especially apt for group study circles; all aim to be useful as spiritual reading for members in every branch of the Movement.

It is our hope and prayer that this series will continue to grow organically under the Holy Spirit's guidance. Some Essays will connect more strongly with our members, and others less, while some may fall by the wayside after their useful moment has passed. Yet perhaps the best

RC Essays will stand the test of time, becoming spiritual and intellectual nourishment for many generations of Movement members.

Please send your ideas and feedback to us through the feedback button at RCSpirituality.org.

INTRODUCTION

In the book of the Prophet Ezekiel (36:2–27) we read:

❝ I will give you a new heart, and a new spirit I will put within you. I will remove the heart of stone from your flesh and give you a heart of flesh. I will put my spirit within you so that you walk in my statutes, observe my ordinances, and keep them. You will live in the land I gave to your ancestors; you will be my people, and I will be your God.

The prophet tells us that if a people is to belong to God, they must begin with a new heart. This heart is not something they have acquired or conquered; it is, rather, a gift. The prophet goes on to say that this new heart alone will enable them to follow God's statutes, ordinances, and rules, and not vice versa; this heart alone will seal them as members of God's people. An interior reality within them, a new heart, will become the very foundation of their identity.

During our renewal process, Regnum Christi members have been asking themselves: can we remove our hearts of stone and receive new hearts? As the prophet implies, we ourselves are not up to the task. It is only when we return God's original gift to us, the spirit that he has imbued in our charismatic family, that he can enable us to do this.

The purpose of this essay is threefold. First, to propose that God's fundamental gift to our Movement is our specific devotion to the Sacred Heart of Jesus. Second, to understand the specific form this devotion takes in the Regnum Christi Movement. Finally, we will explore some practical means for the formation of our hearts according to our supreme model, the Sacred Heart of Jesus.

NOTES

PART I

The Heart of Christ as the Source of the Regnum Christi Movement

"Imple superna gratia, quae tu creasti, pectora."
("Fill with your heavenly grace the hearts that you created.")[2]

To understand anything thoroughly, we must discover its origin. Aristotle was correct to say: *"All men know that to be wise means to deal with the first causes and the principles of things."*[3] This is obvious. It would be wrong to believe, for example, that we could know anyone well without knowing his family and his origins, at least to a certain degree. The same applies to a nation or country; we could not claim to understand it without knowing its history and political birth, and the values and circumstances that accompanied it. The Regnum Christi Movement is not a person nor a nation, but it is a spiritual family, and to understand it we, too, must study its origin. Every community is built upon bedrock principles or moral intuitions; so, too, is the Regnum Christi Movement. A fundamental question must be this: when we search our history and deep inside ourselves, what do we discover to be the bedrock that unites us as a family? What specific ground do we stand upon that is "Regnum Christi ground"?

---

2   From the Hymn *Veni Creator Spiritus*, which the Movement members traditionally sing before their daily meditation: "Fill with your heavenly grace the hearts that you created."

3   Aristotle, *Metaphysics*, A.1.

Perhaps for the Regnum Christi Movement and, for that matter, for the Church in general, it is not a "ground" at all. Nor is it an abstract idea or a value system. Around the 1930s Martin Heidegger proposed for modern, existential society the concept of "ground," *der grund*, as the foundation or first principle which gave solidity and order, and therefore also the strength, for this society to flourish. For him, the best analogy for that which *first* supports human life was the ground, this solid, stable stuff under our feet. Going back 2,000 years, Heraclitus, one of the first important Greek philosophers, proposed that this beginning principle was *logos*, a term signifying a principle of order and knowledge, and, eventually, a reason or logical discourse. For the Greeks, that which best made human life flourish, the *first thing* of everything else, was our *reason*, our ability to think, our true ideas. For them, it wasn't this solid stuff under our feet, but rather this almost airy, spiritual thing, intangible in itself but full of fruitful power, that gave a foundation for everything that was to follow.

The wonderful thing about Christianity, and about Regnum Christi especially, is that our first principle is not a reasonable idea or an order that we can agree upon, nor an existential ground we can stand upon. It is rather *a heart we can lean upon*, just as St. John did during the last Supper. Regnum Christi is based neither on an idea, nor on some kind of natural bedrock, but on a living heart, on a free and loving person, Jesus Christ. Since this is our principle, our first thing, it is by leaning on this heart that we will understand and fulfill our vocation, our mission, as members of Regnum Christi. If the Heart of Christ is the source of Regnum Christi, then it is by knowing it, loving it, and communicating with it that we will arrive to that true "wisdom" (in Aristotle's words) concerning the Movement for which we were looking.[4]

That the Heart of Christ is the source and foundation of Regnum Christi must be demonstrated. Other "origins" of the Movement could be proposed (for example, the person of the founder of the Movement, or the idea of charity, or a manifestation of the Holy Spirit in the rise of new ecclesial lay movements). One could use a historical method, going back to the origins of the Congregation of the Legion of Christ (whose first name was, as we know, "Missionaries of the Sacred Heart and Our Lady of Sorrows"). We could look at the foundation of the Movement in Mexico, and discover how the devotion to the Sacred Heart of Jesus was preeminent in the times of the formation and foundation of Regnum Christi. We could find how this devotion influenced the religious culture, the founder, and the first members of the Legion of Christ, and later how this developed in the first years from the Foundation of Regnum Christi. This would be a historical demonstration, and it would be legitimate. Another method would be to explain this truth theologically or philosophically, a way that we just lightly touched upon, and that would certainly be very fruitful.[5]

For brevity's sake, and in order not to exceed the scope of this essay, we have chosen a third way: to demonstrate the fundamental nature of the devotion to the Sacred Heart of Jesus for the Regnum Christi

---

4   Of course, the Heart of Christ can also be considered the origin of the Church itself and everything in it! We will discuss the specificity of the "Regnum Christi way" of understanding and practicing this devotion in the second section of this essay.

5   For those interested in these two approaches, cfr. Fr. Luis Garza's extensive essay *The Sacred Heart: Center and Source of the Spirituality of the Legion of Christ and the Regnum Christi Movement*, published Nov. 19, 2013, available at Regnumchristi.org.

Movement through a careful reading of its authoritative texts. These will include texts from the written spirituality of the Legionaries of Christ, the Consecrated Women of Regnum Christi, the Consecrated Men of Regnum Christi, and the lay members of Regnum Christi.

A. SPIRITUALITY OF THE LEGIONARIES OF CHRIST

If we were first-time readers of the recently approved Constitutions of the Legionaries of Christ (CLC)[6], what would almost assuredly strike us as one of the specifying notes in the text is that the Sacred Heart of Jesus is the first appellation mentioned in the paragraph dedicated to the "patrons" of the Congregation.[7] Other names follow, but the fact that the Sacred Heart is the first already implies a priority, a kind of inferred source from which all else flows. Equally striking would be the first characteristic of its spirituality, Christ-centeredness: *"Christ-centeredness constitutes the fundamental and specific characteristic of the Legionary spirit."*[8] That line alone already points very clearly to the importance of the Sacred Heart to all Legionaries: Christ-centeredness is the fundamental characteristic of its spirituality (the essential trait, the *sine qua non* of its identity), and the specific one (that which makes it "special," that which differentiates us from other groups).[9]

---

6   Approved in 2014.

7   Constitutions of the Legion of Christ, #7.

8   Constitutions of the Legion of Christ, #8.

9   All groups in the Church could be considered Christ-centered… if not, they would not be Christian! Nevertheless, some groups do insist, for example, more on the spirituality of a saint, or on Marian aspects of the mystery of Christ, or on the Holy Spirit, etc. In this way, Regnum Christi is specifically Christ-centered.

The objection can be made that Christ-centeredness is not exactly devotion to the Sacred Heart. In one sense, this is correct. In fact, the English translation of the Constitutions translates "*culto al*" in Spanish to "devotion to" in English. This was done because today the English word "cult" is ordinarily identified with religious or pagan cults, and not with the original sense of the word, which we find in words like "cultivation,"or "culture." The Chapter Fathers who wrote the text of the new Constitutions in Spanish purposefully changed *devoción á* to *culto al* in their discussions of our relationship with the Sacred Heart. They did this precisely in order to show that what is practiced in the Legion (and in Regnum Christi, for that matter) is not so much devotion to the Sacred Heart in the traditional sense of devotions and prayers, etc., but rather of something more basic: a true "cultivation of" or "interest given to" Jesus Christ. In this sense it is correct to say that Christ-centeredness in the Legion is not the *traditional* devotion to the Sacred Heart, but rather something more fundamental: a new, or deeper way, of understanding this devotion. This is true, and very important.

In another sense, however, we can say that this objection is false. The most recent document from the Holy See concerning the Sacred Heart is the *Directory on Popular Piety and the Liturgy: Principles and Guidelines*, published in 2001 by the Congregation for Divine Worship and the Discipline of the Sacraments. There we read the following (n. 166):

 "Understood in the light of the Scriptures, the term "Sacred Heart of Jesus" denotes the entire mystery of Christ, the totality of his being, and his person considered in its most intimate essential: Son of

God, uncreated wisdom; infinite charity, principal of the salvation and sanctification of mankind. The "Sacred Heart" is Christ, the Word Incarnate.[10]

Understood in this way, as we do in the Movement, Christ-centeredness and devotion to the Sacred Heart are practically synonymous, and we can say our objection has been resolved. In the end, both answers to our original objection tell us the same thing: Christ-centeredness and devotion to the Sacred Heart are fundamentally the same thing when we understand this devotion in the way the Church, and the Movement, ask us to understand it. We will touch upon this later in this essay.

If we read CLC 9, we have a specific number for the devotion to the Sacred Heart: *"In the devotion to (culto al) the Sacred Heart of Jesus, a Legionary has a privileged path to form a meek and humble priestly heart and to spread Christ's Kingdom throughout the world…"* Legionaries who participated in the long process of reviewing our Constitutions will remember when Mgr. de Paolis, the Pontifical Delegate assigned to us for that process, presented to us the first document, a sort of *instrumentum laboris* (a "first draft") for our consideration, which summarized what was thought to be our specific charism. In this document the Sacred Heart was not even mentioned, while Christ the King prominently was.

It was only because of the insistence of the Legionaries

---

10   Congregation for Divine Worship and the Discipline of the Sacraments, *Directory on Popular Piety and the Liturgy*, #166, 2001.

that this was changed.[11] Most Legionaries had the intuition that the Sacred Heart was more fundamental to our spirit than even our obvious love of the title Christ the King. Instead of replacing it or simply forgetting it altogether, which was proposed, we embraced the devotion to the Sacred Heart even more deeply.

Though we cannot do a thorough investigation of all Legionary spirituality texts, it does seem appropriate here to mention number 71 of our recently published "Ratio Institutionis," *Christus Vita Vestra*. In this fundamental publication, the Christocentric spirituality of the Legion is strongly emphasized once again, and in number 71, we read the following:

> The Kingdom of God can be described as the life of the Heart of Christ overflowing into the hearts of his disciples… In this experience of the Kingdom, two lines of our Christocentric spirituality are united: devotion to the Sacred Heart of Jesus… and the devotion to Christ the King… The first devotion nourishes his interior life; the second inspires and expresses his mission.

It is a beautiful text, and helps us to place our Regnum Christi devotion to Christ the King—which finds its most obvious manifestation in our daily motto: "*Thy Kingdom Come!*"—in its proper place. Nevertheless, as far as being a fundamental source of our spirituality, the

---

11   I am speaking here only of this specific discussion within the Legion. As a lay member of Regnum Christi pointed out to me: *"The laity in EVERY territory also insisted on this, which strengthens the case that the principle is charismatic to the Movement, and not merely to the Legion."*

devotion to Christ the King is not on an equal footing with our devotion to the Sacred Heart. The Constitutions themselves precede the number on the "Kingdom of Christ" (number 11) with numbers on Christ-centeredness (number 8), Devotion to the Sacred Heart (number 9), and charity (number 10), and in number 12 we find that the contemplative aspect precedes the militant and evangelizing aspects. *Nemo dat quod non habet* (no one can give what they do not first possess) says the old Latin adage, and if we are to act as soldiers of Christ, we must first be imbued with his spirit, his heart. As has been mentioned many times already, especially in the spiritual life, order is of utmost important.

Already from these brief examples we can begin to see that something in the devotion to the Sacred Heart is at the very source of a Legionary's spirituality: at the source of his life is the Heart of Jesus. But let us move on to consider the spirituality of the Consecrated Women of Regnum Christi.

B. SPIRITUALITY OF THE CONSECRATED WOMEN OF REGNUM CHRISTI

Though there is not a specific number concerning the Sacred Heart in the recently approved Statutes (*ad experimentum*) of the RC Consecrated Women's branch, nevertheless the Sacred Heart is also the first specification concerning Christ that they use to describe their spirituality, and Christ-centeredness is also the first number concerning their specific spirituality. There is a beautiful passage in this number, found only in the Consecrated Women's Statutes, which reads:

A Consecrated Woman fixes her gaze upon the Heart of Christ the King who came to this world to establish his Kingdom... she allows herself to be penetrated by the love of Christ, conforming to his sentiments...[12]

The allusion to the historical and theological link between the Sacred Heart and Christ the King is notable, but the spiritual emphasis is even clearer: the Consecrated Woman looks to the Heart of Christ to understand her vocation. The entire language of this number could be a description of a Sacred Heart devotion as lived among our Consecrated Sisters, and this again seems fundamental.

C. SPIRITUALITY OF THE CONSECRATED MEN OF REGNUM CHRISTI

The newly approved (*ad experimentum*) Statutes of the Consecrated Men of Regnum Christi reveal the same basic structure in their specific spirituality and the place of the Sacred Heart it. In the same manner as the Consecrated Women, the Consecrated Men also do not have a specific number dedicated to the Sacred Heart. Nevertheless, like their Consecrated Sisters, they also place the love of Jesus Christ at the beginning of the first number dedicated to the spirituality of the association. [13]The next two numbers that follow, numbers 9 and 10, are eminently Christocentric, and insist on the Consecrated Man's love for Christ and Christ's "merciful

---

12   Statutes of the Consecrated Women of Regnum Christi, #8.

13   Statutes of the Consecrated Men of Regnum Christi, #8.

love of his Heart."[14] Once again, the devotion to Christ the King is mentioned and underlined,[15] but only once the earlier numbers have already been presented. In our search for order, a recurring pattern can be noted in all the three branches of consecrated life in Regnum Christi: first, Christ-centeredness; second, this Christocentric spirituality expressed through the devotion to his Heart and his love; third, devotion to Christ as King.

D. SPIRITUALITY OF THE LAY MEMBERS OF REGNUM CHRISTI

At the writing of this essay, the General Statutes of Regnum Christi are also still only approved *ad experimentum* (for the time being). Though this text is only a draft, and we can expect modifications before its final version, we can mention two things of note in this essay:

1. The initial prayer.

2. The fact that Christ-centeredness continues to dominate the spectrum of characteristics of Regnum Christi spirituality, especially under the aspect of the love of Christ's Heart.

This is the beginning of the initial prayer in the English translation: "*Lord Jesus, our King and faithful Friend, you have called us to be part of this spiritual family, born from your Heart.*" Though it is a rather free translation of the original in Spanish, nevertheless we can say that it faithfully elucidates the same double approach to the

---

14   Statutes of the Consecrated Men of Regnum Christi, #10.

15   Statutes of the Consecrated Men of Regnum Christi, #11.

mystery of Christ that we found in number 71 of the *Ratio Institutionis*: a spiritual family born from the Heart of Christ that manifests itself in service to Christ known as King. Here again we can see what we have noticed before: whenever our Regnum Christi spirituality addresses Christ the King, it is always after its original recognition of being a Movement "born from your Heart".

The same can be said of the specific spirituality expressed in the Draft. Here again, the first number is very close in spirit and meaning to the similar numbers concerning Christ-centeredness and Devotion to the Sacred Heart that we see in the Consecrated Branches' texts (number 12):

❝The spirituality of Regnum Christi is founded in the contemplation and following of Christ, who reveals the merciful love of his Heart from his Incarnation up to the culminating moment of the Crucifixion and Resurrection, and proclaims and establishes the Kingdom of God.

Immediately following this number is the number on the *Spirituality of the Kingdom*, which is evidence of our devotion to Christ the King, but again it is clear that this call to establish his Kingdom comes from a deeper source: his Heart.[16]

Among the many other texts that we could use, numbers 74 and 75 of the Regnum Christi Member's Handbook

---

16 The fact that the Draft does not specifically mention the Sacred Heart of Jesus can be attributed to many factors. Personally, I believe it is an institutional oversight of a charismatic reality that will be corrected by the definitive Regnum Christi assemblies and in the definitive text, much as it was for the CLC.

are particularly telling.[17] Here again, we find beautiful passages not only of Christ-centeredness as the essential element of RC Spirituality, but also specifically of the Sacred Heart Devotion: *"As an essential part of this Christ-centered spirituality, the Movement instills in its members a true devotion to the Sacred Heart of Jesus…"* Here again we note the essential quality of the Sacred Heart devotion.

E. SOME BRIEF CONCLUSIONS

I believe that this brief analysis of some of the fundamental Regnum Christi texts shows that, at the source and beginning of Regnum Christi, is the Heart of Christ. This is crucial. Understanding and drawing the necessary conclusions from this is extremely important to everything a Regnum Christi member eventually does, in whatever branch, in whatever apostolate. We have already asked with the psalmist *"If foundations are destroyed, what can the just one do?"*[18] and indeed, if the very foundation or source of Regnum Christi is misunderstood, or even worse, ignored, then we cannot hope to escape worse misunderstandings or errors of direction, emphasis, and decision in the future.

Let us take an example in the political world: if the great majority of citizens of the United States of America believe freedom to be their core value, will not every American tend to prize freedom above all other values, and even be ready to sacrifice them, if need be, to preserve freedom? Certainly so. Even if they were mistaken (if, in reality, some other value were to lie even

---

17   Published in 2009.

18   Psalm 11:3.

nearer the foundation of their nation), if freedom were that value that was recognized and proclaimed, then many other values would necessarily be sacrificed for the sake of freedom. The same might be said of the political ideals of a Communist State: for the sake of their core value of a future classless state, many other values would be ignored or even trampled upon. Though the analogy may not be perfect, the same is true of the Regnum Christi Movement: the value we recognize as our fundamental value will necessarily inform and direct all the other values that follow, strengthening some and weakening others. The foundational value of Regnum Christi, however, is not freedom, nor is it classless brotherhood. In fact, if we are correct, it is not even charity, or militancy, or the formation of apostles: it is the Heart of Christ.

NOTES

PART II

What Does "Devotion to the Sacred Heart" Mean to the Member of Regnum Christi?

"Infunde amorem cordibus."
("Infuse love into our hearts.")[19]

The second part of this essay aims to discover what devotion to the Sacred Heart means to a member of Regnum Christi. It may well be true that the Heart of Christ is at the core of Regnum Christi, but what does "the Heart of Christ" actually mean; what is this Sacred *Heart* to which we are supposed to be devoted? There are many possibilities. Is it, for example, just a synonym for Christ-centeredness? Is this "heart" merely a poetic name for the soul? Is it a symbol, for example, of his will, or his intelligence, or maybe even a mix of the two? Is it that physical organ which pumped his divine blood while on earth and still does so in his glorified body? Or do we mean something else by this name?

To answer these questions, once again we could go to a long explanation of the devotion to the Sacred Heart as understood in the Church as it has developed historically, especially in medieval times, and more recently since the revelations of St. Margaret Mary de Alacoque in 17th century France. We could also study the many Papal documents that have been written

---

19   Hymn, *Veni Creator Spiritus.*

about this devotion; Leo XIII, Pius XI, and Pius XII all wrote important encyclicals about the devotion, and all the modern Popes have spoken often of it in other various and noteworthy ways. These methods would be legitimate, and informative, but they are beyond the scope and length of this essay.[20] Let it suffice for us to underline just one explanation of this devotion that sheds light on how we as Regnum Christi members are to understand it. To do this, we return to the Directory[21] we have already mentioned in Part I.

A. MEANING OF "DEVOTION TO THE SACRED HEART"

In the passage from this Directory, we can read again:

❝Understood in the light of the Scriptures, the term "Sacred Heart of Jesus" denotes the entire mystery of Christ, the totality of his being, and his person considered in its most intimate essential:[22] Son of God, uncreated wisdom; infinite charity, principal of the salvation and sanctification of mankind. The "Sacred Heart" is Christ, the Word Incarnate, Saviour, intrinsically containing, in the Spirit, an infinite divine-human love for the Father and for his brothers.[23]

---

20 Once again, I would like to refer readers interested in these approaches to Fr. Luis Garza's essay that we have already mentioned in note # 3 above.

21 Congregation for Divine Worship and the Discipline of the Sacraments, #166, 2001, *Directory on Popular Piety and the Liturgy*.

22 For the term "intimate essential," I was unable to find the corresponding text in Latin. In French it is *le centre intime et essentiel de sa personne*, and in Spanish *su persona considerada en el núcleo más íntimo y esencial*.

23 Congregation for Divine Worship and the Discipline of the Sacraments, #166, 2001. Directory on Popular Piety and the Liturgy, by the Congregation for Divine Worship and the Discipline of the Sacraments, 2001, #166.

According to this, as we have already stated, devotion to the Sacred Heart is simply devotion to Christ, in his entirety. That seems clear enough, but not entirely helpful, since of course all Christians must be devoted to Christ. For those, like we in RC, who claim the Sacred Heart devotion as something essential and fundamental to our spirituality, the question is this: what is *specific* about our devotion to the Sacred Heart? What is it that is different for us from the love and adoration that all Christians owe Jesus Christ?

I think the answers lies in a phrase in the text we just read that mirrors and sheds light upon what we have always practiced in Regnum Christi. The phrase speaks of a sort of distillation of all the elements in the traditional devotion to the Sacred Heart, in order to arrive to the essential ones. We read: *the "Sacred Heart of Jesus" denotes the entire mystery of Christ, the totality of his being, and his person considered in its most intimate essential.* At a first reading, "most intimate essential" seems to include two adjectives without their accompanying noun, but upon examining the texts of other translations, the meaning becomes clear. The Latin text, if it exists, seems to be lacking from the Vatican's website, but the French translation is *le centre intime et essentiel de sa personne (the intimate and essential center of his person)* and the Spanish *su persona considerada en el nucleo más íntimo y esencial (his person considered in its most intimate and essential nucleus.)* It is clear from the Church's latest official document on this Devotion that she understands the Sacred Heart as *that which is most intimate and essential to the person of Jesus Christ.* Of course, we all must imitate Christ, but the Church seems to tell us that her understanding of this devotion implies going to what is most important in his Person. The implication is that the person who is devoted to the Sacred Heart will not have to worry too much about the things that were not essential to Jesus: the clothes he wore, the length of his hair, or even his physical strength and endurance. These were part of who he was, but they were not essential. We could even say the same about his amazing force of will and his unique intelligence. If all these characteristics, however, are not what is most intimate and essential to the person of Jesus Christ, what is? What do we need to focus on, as we look into his Heart? The answer seems so simple that perhaps it easily escapes us. What is most intimate and essential to the person of Jesus is, obviously, his love.

When we recognize this, and accept it, a revealing light seems to come over the Regnum Christi Movement. For if this is true, in this one flash of light we can recognize and know what must be the specific characteristic of our devotion to the Sacred Heart of Jesus: to be devoted to the love of the Heart of Jesus Christ, and to strive above all to imitate Jesus in the way He loved. This, of course, must mean also to strive to think like him, to practice determination like him, to be faithful like him. But for the sake of clarity and order, we arrive at the very foundations of Regnum Christi spirituality through our effort to love like him. It is our centripetal point, from which we can begin to unequivocally march forward and outward in the development of our Movement and its apostolates. The Regnum Christi member who strives to live this and puts it first in his or her spiritual program cannot fail to be on the best path possible. This is what makes it possible for us to begin to "*remove the heart of stone from our flesh and give us a heart of flesh.*"[24]

---

24   Ezekiel 36:2–27.

If one had lingering doubts concerning this, an examen of conscience applying the old rule of trial and error would be revealing. If in our past personal lives Christ's love was not the first and most powerful motivation for our actions and apostolates, that which we tried to imitate in all that we did, what happened? Did we not run into consequences from our past apostolic works that puzzled us? Did we not find that perhaps, almost unknowingly, we had become somewhat hard-hearted, with apostolates that were not working as they should, and with stagnation in our spiritual and apostolic lives? The fruitfulness of Regnum Christi did not in the past, nor does it now, depend on our faithfulness to the human ideas of a human founder, any abstract idea, or a methodology; Regnum Christi's fruitfulness depends principally on each member's union with the human and divine *love* of Jesus Christ.

Understood by the Church, *this* is the meaning of the devotion to the Sacred Heart of Jesus, at least in its deepest sense. For us specifically as Regnum Christi members -and this is a wonderful aspect of this truth- it is also the meaning of *our* devotion to the Sacred Heart. Historically the Movement has always understood the Sacred Heart Devotion to be fundamentally a devotion to the *love* of Jesus Christ, to that which is most essential in Him. Most members will remember this by the distinction that we habitually made between "devotions" and "Devotion," and how we were habitually encouraged to strive for the latter. Nevertheless, however present this was to us during certain historical moments in our past, there were also moments when it was misunderstood, or even ignored. Today, to recognize this source of our spirituality and accept it, personally and institutionally, would be to return fruitfully to the Regnum Christi path. The love of Christ should be the sun around which Regnum Christi orbits, the source from which it draws its strength, and the ideal towards which it always strives.

Under the guise or even *disguise* of a more traditional understanding of the devotion to the Sacred Heart, and the confusion that surrounded the hierarchy of other Regnum Christi virtues, the priority of our devotion to the Lord's Heart probably has, in most instances, not been fully lived. When we understand the devotion to the Sacred Heart as something other than *this* devotion, or when we understand as the source of our spirituality some other characteristic (for example, the formation of apostles), then we are losing our specific way. Practicing the nine First Fridays devotion to the Sacred Heart can be very fruitful, as can be the enthroning of an icon of the Sacred Heart in our homes, but these are not the most essential practices in our attention to Christ. In a similar way, surely we must form apostles, but if we do not do this soundly grounded first in the love of Christ, we will soon run into problems.

To be devoted to the Sacred Heart in this way is not always easy to grasp. In his great encyclical *God is Love*, Pope Benedict XVI masterfully shows how rich and equivocal the word "love" is in English and other modern languages, and how this can lead to confusion. Nevertheless, the Pope shows how "*fundamentally, love is a single reality, but with different dimensions;*"[25] how God's love is at the same time Eros and Agape; and how Christ is "*a lover with all the passion of a true love.*"[26] Love is not

---

25   Pope Benedict XVI, *Deus Caritas Est*, #8.

26   Pope Benedict XVI, *Deus Caritas Est*, #10.

just an act of the will (as so often read, even in the best of Catholic authors) but rather the singular reality of the love in the Heart of Christ. Though this love does include willing as one of its dimensions, it also goes beyond it: it includes passion, suffering, and tenderness. It includes and presupposes our affectivity. It is multi-dimensional.

B. MEANING OF THE "HEART"

What then really is this *Heart?* For if we have now discovered what "Sacred Heart" fundamentally means *(the most intimate and essential nucleus of the Person of Jesus Christ),*[27] and what that implies for us *(a true devotion to the "love" of Jesus Christ),*[28] we still must try to understand what this Heart really *is* in order to be able to form it. To know that it is the most essential and intimate nucleus of Jesus' person is important, but its metaphysical reality remains somewhat hidden. The *Catechism of the Catholic Church* (2563) tells us that when the Bible uses the word "heart" it is speaking of a hidden center in ourselves of utmost importance:

The heart is the dwelling-place where I am, where I live; according to the Semitic or Biblical expression, the heart is the place "to which I withdraw." The heart is our hidden center, beyond the grasp of our reason and of others; only the Spirit of God can fathom the human heart and know it fully. The heart is the place of decision, deeper than our psychic drives. It is the place of truth, where we choose life or death. It is the place of encounter, because

---

27 The most intimate and essential nucleus of the Person of Jesus Christ.

28 A true devotion to the "love" of Jesus Christ.

as image of God we live in relation: it is the place of covenant.

This being so, how can we form something which is so mysterious, so hidden, and so beyond "our reason and others"? To answer this question, we will make a brief excursus into traditional and modern Christian anthropology.

In traditional Christian anthropology, man has but two spiritual faculties: the intelligence and the will. In this understanding of man, the will is the spiritual center of our decision-making, and our intelligence is the spiritual center of our thinking. But looking at the Heart of Christ, something seems to be missing here. If the most intimate and essential center of his person is his heart, and this is not contained within the domains of either of our two spiritual faculties, then what status does this heart, or even love for that matter, have? The question is *What was the spiritual center of Jesus' loving?* and therefore, *What is the spiritual center of our loving?* A 20th century philosopher and theologian, Dietrich Von Hildebrand, claimed that according to classic and scholastic anthropology, the heart was relegated to a sub-rational and thus sub-spiritual level.

> According to Aristotle, the intellect and the will belong to the rational part of man; the affective realm, and with it the heart, belong to the irrational part in man, that is, to the area of experience which man allegedly shares with the animals.[29]

---

29   Dietrich Von Hildebrand, "*The Heart*," page 4, St. Augustine Press, 2007.

This puzzled him. Essentially it was by means of his own meditations on the Heart of Christ that Von Hildebrand arrived to the conclusion that there had to be something else, something that could be posited as the spiritual center of affectivity, clearly distinct from the will and the intelligence. This presupposed what we lightly touched upon before: that love is not simply an act of the will or of the intellect. When we read a text like the aforementioned "the Consecrated Woman should experience a personal, real, passionate, and faithful love of Christ," clearly this describes a spiritual experience, an experience you cannot realize with just your head or your will. You need something else. Von Hildebrand would say that this something else is your "heart." This is neither the heart as synonymous with the soul, nor the heart as the physical organ we all possess, but rather, the heart understood as a third spiritual faculty, the spiritual center of our affectivity.[30] Therefore, just as the will is the spiritual center of our decision-making and the intelligence is the spiritual source of our reasoning, Von Hildebrand posits the heart as the spiritual center of our affective responses.

---

30 Other philosophical formulations could be proposed besides those of Von Hildebrand. For example, a very worthwhile system proposed by the Catholic psychologist Conrad Baars would define the "heart" as "the intimate association of our humane emotions with our intuitive mind." (*Feeling and Healing Your Emotions*, page 75) The point here is not to propose any particular philosophical system, but to give the heart all the metaphysical and spiritual weight that existentially it exercises in our daily lives.

Love (as well as other responses such as enthusiasm and compassion) is considered one of its responses, and its most important.[31]

If we accept this, then the meaning of the devotion to the Sacred Heart becomes much clearer. Since at least medieval times, the Church and its saints have intuitively used the heart as the symbol or the source of love, not the head, nor the will. The saints felt no need of philosophical distinctions. Their devotion to the Sacred Heart of Jesus developed organically with a unique spiritual intuition: wanting to love as Jesus loved, and to love Him for loving us in such an extraordinary way. It is quite wonderful, therefore, to discover that their spiritual intuition, Von Hildebrand's philosophical work, the Church's most recent authoritative texts, and our own experience with the Regnum Christi movement all point to the same reality. We live our devotion to the Sacred Heart of Jesus in striving to experience the love of Jesus Christ, and striving to live this love in the way He did.

---

31   We are only too aware of the difficulties of proposing a third spiritual faculty as a serious philosophical concept, and it would certainly be beyond the scope of this essay to delve into its many implications. For example, it would be necessary to distinguish between spiritual feelings and non-spiritual ones (which we obviously do share with many members of the animal kingdom). It would also be necessary to clarify how to categorize this new faculty alongside the more traditional concepts of the "rational appetite" and the "sensual appetite" of the soul. Normally, a member of Regnum Christi, especially the consecrated branches, would be more familiar with the philosophical distinctions noted by Fr. Ramon Lucas, LC: (Man Incarnate Spirit, page 211): "*The division of psychical activities into two general types, cognitive and tendential, has prevailed... From the point of view of the faculties, this division has been retained, because there is no faculty of feeling distinct from the faculties of knowledge and tendency.*" But to delve into this would demand another entire essay, at least, and would necessarily include many technical philosophical concepts and discussions that seem to this author to be outside the realm of a Regnum Christi Essay. Any commentaries or clarifications concerning these issues, nevertheless, would be appreciated.

This reflection naturally leads us into the third part of this essay.

NOTES

PART III

Practical Implications of the Sacred Heart Devotion in Our Regnum Christi Life

"Oh Lux beatissima, reple cordis intima tuorum fidelium."
("O most blessed Light, fill the inmost heart of your faithful.")[32]

A renewed practice of the Sacred Heart Devotion would have many implications for a member of Regnum Christi. In order to stay within the scope of a RC essay, let us just choose two:

1. Affective formation in the Regnum Christi Movement.

2. Some practical applications and suggestions within our spirituality and traditions.

A. AFFECTIVE FORMATION IN THE REGNUM CHRISTI MOVEMENT

Certainly one of the most obvious implications of this devotion would be a renewed interest in the affective formation of members of the Movement. In the language we have used here, this means attention to the formation of the "heart" as the spiritual center of our affectivity, in order to conform it more perfectly to the Heart of Christ. This increased awareness and attention to the affective formation of the Regnum Christi member (especially in the Consecrated branches) already has

---

32   Hymn *Veni Sancte Spiritus*, fifth stanza: "O most blessed Light, fill the inmost heart of your faithful."

begun, as can be seen by the extensive discussions on the topic in, for example, the new *Ratio Institutionis* of the Legionaries.[33]

What means would be most helpful in assuring the formation of the heart? We do not wish nor pretend to repeat what is already present in so many excellent Regnum Christi texts on the subject. As a complement to these texts, however, we would like to take as a starting point the advice of St. Paul in his letter to the Philippians 4:8:

> Finally, brothers, whatever is true, whatever is honorable, whatever is just, whatever is pure, whatever is lovely, whatever is gracious, if there is any excellence and if there is anything worthy of praise, think about these things.

In all of our daily tasks, duties, decisions, joys, and sufferings, St. Paul encourages us to strive to accomplish and experience those things that truly bring good into our lives, and to train our heart by habitual practice to rejoice in responding to their true values. In his own way, St. Paul proposes a humanistic program of formation that would permit the heart to become the "generous and good" heart Jesus spoke of in Luke 8:15; to be the "excellent soil" in which the Word and grace of God could fall.[34]

---

33   Cfr. *Ratio Institutionis* Chapter 3, Dimension C, 6; Chapter 3, Dimension E; Chapter 3, Dimension F, etc.

34   Luke 8:15: "But as for the seed that fell on rich soil, they are the ones who, when they have heard the word, embrace it with a generous and good heart, and bear fruit through perseverance." Luke uses the Greek words "kale" for our translation's "rich soil," and "kale" and "agathe" for what our translation renders as "a generous and good heart." What is important to note is that the soil, and the heart, are not only morally good (agathos), but also excellent, generous, noble, and beautiful (kalos). In Homer's Iliad, Achilles was the archetypal Greek hero endowed with "kalos."

The lesson is clear: without this type of heart, a Christian's fruitfulness would be drastically impaired.

In this sense, an important implication of an authentic devotion to the Sacred Heart would be a renewed interest in those means that form the heart directly and intuitively, without passing primarily through the intellect or the will. Here we propose three means.

FIRST: The first area would be the effort to habituate oneself to listen to and appreciate good music. After prayer, there are few occupations more efficacious at forming our hearts than listening to truly great music. Though it be beyond the scope of this essay to argue in favor of this statement, for now suffice it to say that music is:

1. The art closest by its nature to the fundamentals of human existence.

2. A wordless expression or articulation of man's existential self, of man's journey towards self-realization, in what is good.

Since this journey is never predetermined, but always under the healthy influence of a good formation or threatened by the powers of error and pride, music plays a powerful part in this life-long struggle. Plato has rightly said that "musical training is a more potent instrument than any other, because rhythm and harmony find their way into the inward places of the soul... imparting grace, and making the soul of him who is rightly educated graceful, or of him who is ill-educated ungraceful."[35]

Despite this, it is amazing to see how lightly we take the whole theme of music, even when we see its overwhelming popularity and power especially among the young. Pop and rock singers are arguably the greatest "stars" in our media-driven world today. The power of their influence is undeniable. But if the musical articulation with which they inundate us includes shallow contentment with what is easily available, or the rejection of order, or the denial of man's higher goals, etc., then we can be sure that the influence on our hearts must be damaging, if not devastating. We can repeat with unerring accuracy what Plato wrote in the *Republic* long ago: " I believe... that when modes of music change, the fundamental laws of the State always change with them."[36] The great Thomistic philosopher Josef Pieper assessed our present situation accurately.

❝I agree with the disturbing observation equating the history of Western music with the history of a soul's degeneration, and I do this with great alarm, aware that music lays bare man's inner existential condition, while this same inner condition receives from music the most direct impulses, for better or worse.[37]

Few things touch and form the heart so immediately as music, and nevertheless music that deforms the

---

35   Plato, The Republic, Book III.

36   Plato, The Republic, Book IV.

37   Josef Pieper, "*Only the Lover Sings: Art and Contemplation*," chapter titled "*Thoughts about Music*."

heart is astonishingly easily permitted in our culture and in the practical education of our youth. If we want to form Christian hearts, music must play its proper role. A discussion of what kind of music is formative or deformative is once again beyond the scope of this essay, so perhaps we can simply claim that few things are more positively formative for a human heart than learning to listen to, enjoy, and appreciate Bach, Mozart, and Beethoven. The list could go on and on, and those to be included in the list could be endlessly debated. Such a list could also include contemporary music. Let it just be said that whatever music we permit on our list should be able to withstand the interrogative fire of Philippians 4:8.

SECOND: A second area to be cultivated would be that of good literature. Few things should be more obvious. If we imbibe great literature, there is no doubt that the formative values and human circumstances portrayed there will become part of our way of responding affectively. Once one has tasted Homer or Tolstoy, it is almost impossible to return to superficial, cheap literature, however exciting or titillating it may be. Our heart was created and structured to respond to the greatest values; there it finds its truest and most enriching enjoyment and peace. But if it is denied these, it will necessarily look for the "easy" responses. As Ryan N. S. Topping wrote in his excellent book *Rebuilding Catholic Culture*:

❝The heart, like some lonely wolf, trots across the vast and barren plains of our nights and days looking for God, scratching under every shiny stone.[38]

One of the first things responsible parents can do to ensure the Christian education of their children is to make sure they become readers of great literature. Here again, as in music, it would be nearly impossible to make a definitive list of formative literary works, and even if it were possible, those included in it would be hotly debated. A good general norm must always be what we have already discussed: does this work help me to conform my heart to the Heart of Jesus by putting my heart in touch with authentic values and ennobling affections? Does it help make my heart into the beautiful and good soil of Luke 8:15? At the risk of promoting my own personal favorites, I believe any list of great and formative literary works must include Homer, Dante, Cervantes, Shakespeare, and Tolstoy (all are demanding, but extremely rewarding). Other more contemporary works that would also be fruitful include those by such authors as Tolkien, Claudel, and Waugh.

THIRD: Finally, we should speak briefly of the visual arts, where painting, sculpture, and—especially today—cinema, have their pride of place. As in music and literature, here also the argument holds that beauty touches and forms our hearts more immediately than does logical argumentation. Thus Christian art must reflect in some way the true beauty of the created world, and make it more accessible to the human heart. Josef Pieper, in his aforementioned book, says:

---

38   R. S. Topping, *Rebuilding Catholic Culture*, Chapter 4, "On Sacraments: when the World is Enchanted."

To see things is the first step toward that primordial and basic mental grasping of reality, which constitutes the essence of man as a spiritual being.[39]

If this is true, then the visual arts have much to do with forming us to see the God-given beauty and goodness in the world. If they do not do that, if they seek to exalt chaos, irrationality, or even the absence of beauty as its theme, then these arts, like bad music, are not forming but deforming the heart. The same criteria we have used for judging music and literature are also legitimate here: those works that build up what is Christian in our hearts should be promoted; those that are dubious should be rejected. Recommendations? Among painters I would suggest that Da Vinci, Raphael, Michelangelo, Rembrandt, Velazquez, and el Greco are among the recognized masters, though I must confess a personal love of many of the works of the French impressionists. Among sculptors, my favorites are Donatello, Michelangelo, Bernini, Rodin, Canova, and the relatively unknown but thrilling Camille Claudel. And movies? Instead of the habitual contemporary fare of thriller, action, and over-sentimental movies, why not watch—at least every once in a while—those films that can edify and teach us? We all know the contemporary overtly Christian movies, like "Facing the Giants" and "A Walk to Remember," but others, less overtly faith-based, are also extremely formative and enjoyable: "Babette's Feast" (one of Pope Francis' favorites), "A Man for All Seasons" (Bishop Robert Barron's favorite movie), "Fiddler on the Roof," "The Sound of Music" (one of my favorites!), "Les Miserables," "Breakfast at

---

39   Josef Pieper, *Only the Lover Sings: Art and Contemplation*, chapter titled "Learning How to See Again."

Tiffany's," "Casablanca," "Schindler's List," "Gone with the Wind," "The Great Gatsby," "West-Side Story," "It's a Wonderful Life," and even such fun stuff like "Tangled" are just a few that we can mention here.[40]

B. SOME PRACTICAL APPLICATIONS AND SUGGESTIONS WITHIN OUR SPIRITUALITY AND TRADITIONS

Beside its implications in the field of affective formation, an authentic devotion to the Sacred Heart will also affect other aspects of our Regnum Christi life. Here we propose a few aspects, without pretending to exhaust its many fecund and perhaps even undiscovered applications.

FIRST: A first thing that devotion to the Sacred Heart could positively affect would be something very simple: our daily vocal prayers. A basic daily Regnum Christi prayer could be something like this: *Sacred Heart of Jesus, make my heart more like yours.* The original form of that prayer was at the end of the traditional litany of the Sacred Heart: *Jesus, meek and humble of heart, make my heart more like yours.* Here we prefer the more basic version for the same reasons mentioned before; that is, to avoid implying that meekness or humility might be our "first" virtue. Our first virtue should always be to strive to love like Christ, and then all the other virtues will follow. Here we can also remember that this prayer does not ask us to act in every situation in the same way as Christ would have acted (as the popular "*What Would Jesus Do?*" bracelets imply). Jesus did many things that would

---

40   Other art forms could be included here, such as ballet or opera. Limitations of length preclude a discussion of these themes, but the same criteria of judgment should be applied.

be impossible for us today (many aspects of his everyday life, as well as many of his miracles), and accomplished many other things that for us would be morally incorrect or imprudent (the Crucifixion itself, the expulsion of demons, etc.). What this prayer implies is for us to act in the spirit of Christ, to act in a way that would always be pleasing to Christ. To conform our heart to that which would be pleasing to the Heart of Christ would be the summit of the formation of the Christian heart.

SECOND: A second aspect related to the first would be to concentrate on Christ-centered prayer in our daily meditation. Be this meditation or contemplation, spiritual reading or adoration, the person of Christ should habitually be our subject. God is the ultimate agent of our sanctification, but as far as we are concerned, prayer is the primary way we have of transforming ourselves according to God's will. If then our devotion to the love of Jesus' Heart is fundamental to us, our prayer should support and nourish this fundamental Regnum Christi ideal. Obviously, the Eucharist and the Gospel should be indispensable paths in our Christ-centered prayer.

THIRD: A third aspect would be, of course, a new and renewed effort to form ourselves in charity. Little wonder that charity has always been the primary virtue for a Regnum Christi member. Indeed, the very fact that it has been first points to its original source, the Heart of Christ. A more intentional devotion to the Sacred Heart should also move us to a greater cultivation of the great virtue of charity.

One dimension of this spiritual work to achieve charity would be to overcome *hard-heartedness*. In Romans 1:29–31, St. Paul makes a list of the sins of the pagans that should be exiled from a Christian's life. He includes *every form of wickedness, evil, greed, and malice; envy, murder, rivalry, treachery, spite, gossips, scandal makers, the insolent, haughty, boastful, and the rebellious toward parents; the senseless, faithless, heartless, and ruthless.* This "heartlessness" in the last line is the Greek word "*astorges*," which means "without *storge*." "*Storge*" in Greek is not *agape*, Christian charity, nor *philos*, friendship love, nor even *eros*, romantic love, but another Greek word for love that signifies merely natural or instinctual affection, like that we see between parents and children (interestingly enough, it could even be applied to the affection we feel for our pets or our favorite sports team). In his book *The Four Loves*, C.S. Lewis dedicates an entire chapter to it, and he translates it as "affection." Although St. Paul always fought against the lack of Christian charity in the early communities, in this passage he also rejects hard-heartedness. It manifests itself in the person who lacks natural affection, is unsociable, unmannerly, impolite, or imprudent. This happens very often even without bad intention or bad will, but this is precisely because hard-heartedness is not a question of will; it is a question of the heart.

The question of "hard-heartedness" is especially important in the Movement because strangely enough, despite our renewal, this many-headed hydra still can and does arise within the Movement today. This very well could be because of wounds received in the past: perhaps because of the disappointing revelations concerning the life of the founder of the Movement, perhaps because of other subtle or not too subtle deviations from an evangelical spirit in the Legionary, Consecrated, or Lay branches. It could also be an over-reaction to our previous rule of never criticizing. Nevertheless, the Sacred Heart Devotion encourages us to love as Jesus loved, with the characteristics of his heart, and—let us say it bluntly—Jesus was never hard-hearted. If at times we find this manifestation in ourselves or in our section for any reason, it is not a good reaction, because it is not a reaction that would proceed from Jesus' Heart.

One example of cultivating more "*storge*" or affection in the Movement would be to renew our confidence in the other members of the Movement, especially in those who do not belong to our specific branch. There is a beautiful passage in E.M. Forster's masterpiece, *Howard's End*, in which the protagonist sisters are talking about their father. It goes like this:

> You remember 'rent.' It was one of father's words—rent to the ideal, to his own faith in human nature. You remember how he would trust strangers, and if they fooled him he would say: "It's better to be fooled than to be suspicious"—that the confidence trick is the work of man, but the want-of-confidence trick is the work of the devil.[41]

"Better to be fooled than to be suspicious." If their father was willing to do this for strangers, should not we be willing to do this with members of our Regnum Christi family?

FOURTH: A fourth and final application concerns something that may seem surprising, but, as we noted in the above section on affective formation, is probably

---

41   E.M. Forster, *Howard's End*, Chapter 5.

quite important. In the Directory that we have already mentioned several times, we read the following about the iconography of the devotion to the Sacred Heart.[42]

Popular piety tends to associate a devotion with its iconographic expression. This is a normal and positive phenomenon. Inconveniences can sometimes arise: iconographic expressions that no longer respond to the artistic taste of the people can sometimes lead to a diminished appreciation of the devotion's object... This can sometimes arise with devotion to the Sacred Heart, with, for example, certain over-sentimental images that are incapable of giving expression to the devotion's robust theological content... Recent times have seen the development of images representing the Sacred Heart of Jesus at the moment of crucifixion which is the highest expression of the love of Christ. The Sacred Heart is Christ crucified, his side pierced by the lance, with blood and water flowing from it (cf, John 19:34).

We mention this as a possible application of our Sacred Heart Devotion because the iconography of our Movement should express in the best way possible the specificity of our devotion to the Heart of Christ, our devotion to his love.

However, as this document says: "*the highest expression of the love of Christ is the Sacred Heart of Christ crucified, his side pierced by a lance...*" Pope Benedict XVI wrote

---

42   Congregation for Divine Worship and the Discipline of the Sacraments, #173, *Directory on Popular Piety and the Liturgy*, 2001.

similarly in *Deus Caritas Est*, 12:

❝By contemplating the pierced side of Christ, we can understand… God is love… It is from there that our definition of love must begin. In this contemplation the Christian discovers the path along which his life and love must move.

If this is true, would not an image representing Christ Crucified, with his heart pierced, be much more appropriate, much more precise, and much more illuminative for us than our traditional "Legionary Christ"? *The Head of Christ* by Warner Sallman has become quite iconic for us, and perhaps many members of the Movement like it, but there are no scars on his forehead, nor spittle on his face. In fact, is not Sallman's Christ almost the contrary artistic image of what we mean when we strive to live our devotion to the love of Jesus' Heart, which finds its highest expression in his Crucified love?

The point is arguable. Nevertheless, it seems that this could be another example of how we have, in all good will, concentrated on elements of Jesus that are good —his nobility, his serenity—but not on what is essential to him, and to us: his love. Perhaps a Crucifixion with his Pierced Heart such as those by Zurbaran, van Dyck, or Velazquez[43] (my favorite) would more artistically portray this highest expression of his love. Besides, in these images one will find nobility and serenity, to an almost miraculous degree.

---

43   The author admits that he made this change many years ago in his office in a small town in France.

NOTES

CONCLUSION

In this essay, we have tried to focus on what is truly fundamental and essential for our Regnum Christi spirituality. This essay proposes that the Heart of Christ is the source and origin of the Regnum Christi Movement, and that our specific devotion to the Sacred Heart is an indispensable "first thing" among our many priorities and ideals. In the last section of the essay we investigated several more practical applications of this principle, and ended with elements such as the iconography used in our Movement which, though it is important, is certainly not the most fundamental element. So let us end this essay with two quotations that return us to our foundations. The first is from Romano Guardini's "The Lord," and it mirrors precisely what this essay proposes is specific and of primary importance in our RC spirituality:

❝ If anyone should ask: "what is certain in life and death—so certain that everything else may be anchored in it?", the answer is: the love of Christ. Life teaches us that this is the only true reply. Not people—not even the best and dearest; not science, or philosophy, or art or any other product of human genius. Also not nature, which is so full of profound deception; neither time nor fate… Not even simply "God"; for his wrath has been roused by sin, and how without Christ would we know what to expect from him? Only Christ's love is certain. We cannot even say God's love; for that God loves us we also know, ultimately, only through Christ. And even if we did know without Christ that God loved us—

love can also be inexorable, and the more noble it is, the more demanding. Only through Christ do we know that God's love is forgiving. Certain is only that which manifested itself on the Cross. What has been said so often and so inadequately is true: The Heart of Jesus Christ is the beginning and end of all things.[44]

That love of Christ, that Heart, is also specifically the beginning and end of our RC spirituality.

The second is from one of my favorite novels of the 20th century, *Brideshead Revisited*, by Evelyn Waugh. In the Epilogue, given the same title as the entire book, Charles Ryder, now in the army during World War II, finds himself back in the aristocratic castle of Brideshead with his brigade. As he enters the mansion, he describes himself to his aide as "homeless, childless, middle-aged, and love-less". The state of the mansion is much like the state of his soul: abandoned during many years, its one-time splendor now in ruins, a revered place now overrun by the soldiers and the banal necessities of the war. But as he rummages through this building that was the home of the best years of his life, Ryder, a new convert to Catholicism, goes to visit the last room he had not visited, the chapel. Spiritually suffering, he says a prayer before the tabernacle, and he notices there, still after all those years, the faithful red tabernacle light burning. On leaving the chapel, he reflects:

*The builders did not know the uses to which their

---

44   Romano Guardini, *The Lord*, Romano Guardini, part 54, chapter XIV, Jesus' Death.

work would descend; year by year, generation after generation, they enriched and extended it… But then came this age, and all their work was brought to nothing: vanity of vanities, all is vanity… And yet that is not the last word; it is not even an apt word: it is a dead word. Something quite remote from anything the builders intended has come out of their work, and out of the fierce little human tragedy in which I played; something none of us thought about at the time; a small red flame… the flame which the old knights saw from their tombs, which they saw put out; that flame burns again for other soldiers, far from home, farther, in heart, than Acre or Jerusalem. It could not have been lit but for the builders and the tragedians, and there I found it this morning, burning anew among the old stones.[45]

I feel this is a very beautiful image for us also in Regnum Christi. What we are given to live today could not have been "lit" but for the builders and the tragedians of our Regnum Christi past, even if this was not always what they first intended. Still, beautifully "*burning anew among the old stones*,"what is given to us to rediscover today is the red flame burning before the Eucharist, symbol of the Heart of Christ.

---

45   Evelyn Waugh, *Brideshead Revisited*, Epilogue.

PRACTICAL EXAM ON DEVOTION TO THE SACRED HEART

1. What do I consider the fundamental characteristic of my Regnum Christi spirituality?

2. In what circumstances of my life have I felt that I needed the gift of a "new heart" from the Lord? What concrete means could I consciously try to apply in order to collaborate with his grace to obtain it?

3. What aspects of Jesus' personality most attract me? Do I agree that his most sublime aspect is his love, or are there others aspects that attract me more and which I feel called to imitate?

4. Practically, how do I try to form my heart? Have I ever considered a program that includes music, literature, art, and cinema?

5. If I do a simple conscience exam of my behavior in the past few years, when could I say I have been hard-hearted towards others? How can I work to overcome this?

QUESTIONS FOR SMALL-GROUP STUDY SESSION

1. What is the one aspect of Regnum Christi life that we believe most distinguishes us as a spiritual family?

2. The essay proposes the Devotion to the Sacred Heart as the fundamental source of Regnum Christi and its spirituality. Do we agree? If not, what other aspect of our spirituality or charism do we think it might be?

3. How have we practically practiced the Devotion to the Sacred Heart in our section, team, or personal life, up to now? Have traditional devotions related to this devotion helped us to grow in a deeper understanding of the Heart of Christ?

4. What means proposed in this essay might we practice as a group in order to better form our hearts? What other means can we think of that would perhaps help us more?

5. In general, is our prayer, both vocal and mental, Christ-centered? What books or texts might we propose to other Regnum Christi members that would help them to center their prayer more on Christ?

6. Try to detect some manifestations of hard-heartedness, lack of confidence, or suspicion that have arisen in our section or team. How might we fight against these?

NOTES

EXPLORING MORE

Please visit our website, *RCSpirituality.org* for more spiritual resources, and follow us on Facebook for regular updates: *facebook.com/RCSpirituality*

RC Essays are a service of Regnum Christi.
RegnumChristi.org

Produced by Coronation.
CoronationMedia.com

Developed & self-published by RCSpirituality.
RCSpirituality.org

Made in the USA
Las Vegas, NV
14 September 2023